How to Love You: The God Within

A Woman's Guide to Loving God and Self

Pamela Muhammad

ISBN-13: 978-1537263021

ISBN-10: 1537263021

How to Love You: The God Within

A Woman's Guide to Loving God and Self

Printed in the United States of America.

First Edition, 2016

Authored by Pamela Muhammad

Cover Layout Pamela Muhammad

"In each one of us Allah (God) has placed a certain gift, the fulfillment of which causes us to make our contribution to the whole. Since Allah (God) is the Giver of all gifts and the Nourisher of us all unto perfection, it is only proper that He be acknowledged as the True Center of our existence. If He directs a path, then it will ultimately lead to Him. His Attributes are perfect, His are the Best of names. This means that with His direction, we will achieve excellence in whatever field we choose."

---The Honorable Minister Louis Farrakhan

A Special Note of Gratitude

"Jesus saith unto him, I am the way, the truth, and the life: no man cometh unto the Father, but by me." John 14:6, (KJV)

I thank Allah for His intervention in our affairs in the Person of Master Fard Muhammad, to whom all praise is due forever. I can never thank Allah enough for the Eternal Leader of the Nation of Islam, The Most Honorable Elijah Muhammad, The Living Exalted Christ. And I further thank Allah for blessing us with our Divine Teacher, Guide and Grace in our midst, the Honorable Minister Louis Farrakhan.

Dedication

"Honor thy Father and thy mother: that thy days may be long upon the land which the Lord thy God giveth thee." Exodus 20:12 (KJV)

I dedicate this book to my Beloved parents Yolanda Pride and Jerry Adams. Thank you for assisting Allah (God) in birthing me into this world. I love you very much. I wish I could erase all the pain you have endured in this lifetime. May Allah (God) bless you abundantly.

Acknowledgements

The Most Honorable Elijah Muhammad and The Honorable Minister Louis Farrakhan have been chosen by Allah (God) to lay the foundation for a new world. The foundation for a new world must begin with a new woman. They have been devoted to the elevation of the woman and for this I am very grateful.

I am thankful for The First lady of the Nation of Islam, Mother Khadijah Farrakhan and the great sacrifice she and her family have made.

I am thankful for Mother Tynetta Muhammad, Sister Ava Muhammad, and Sister Donna Farrakhan. These women have been wonderful examples of women in the ministry and have been a great inspiration to me.

I am thankful for Sister Sandy Muhammad, the M.G.T. and G.C.C Captain of the Nation of Islam. She is a great example of an M.G.T. and strong soldier in Islam. Our Muslim Girls Training and General Civilization Class is AMAZING!!!

I am thankful for Sister A'ishah Muhammad, the National Auditing Coordinator of the Nation of Islam who shares wonderful guidance and great wisdom.

I am thankful for Sister Audrey Muhammad who featured my article "Embracing the New You" in her Virtue Magazine in 2014.

I am thankful for Sister Robin Muhammad (Phoenix, AZ) and Sister Najah Muhammad (Cleveland, Oh) who have always been genuine and kind sisters to me.

I am thankful for Sister Lakisa Muhammad (New Orleans, LA), Brother Ventress Hunter (New Orleans, LA) and Cathy Galbreath (Cleveland, Oh) who helped me in a great time of need. May Allah (God) bless you abundantly!

I am thankful for Sister Barbara Muhammad (Cleveland, Oh) who always encouraged me to stay prayerful, and keep Allah at the center.

I am thankful for my family. I pray that Allah (God) will bless you all with the best of health and happiness!

Table of Contents

Introduction

Duty to Allah (God) is First and Foremost

I thank Allah for His intervention in our affairs in the Person of Master Fard Muhammad, to Whom all praise is due forever. I can never thank Allah enough for the Eternal Leader of the Nation of Islam, The Most Honorable Elijah Muhammad, The Living Exalted Christ. And I further thank Allah for blessing us with our Divine Teacher, Guide and Grace in our midst, the Honorable Minister Louis Farrakhan. For if it was not for these men I would not have anything to say.

In the Qur'an Surah 4, titled *Al-Nisa* – **THE WOMEN**, chapter 1 verse 1 reads, *"O people, keep your duty to your Lord, Who created you from a single being and created its mate of the same (kind) and spread from these two, many men and women. And keep your duty to Allah, by Whom you demand one of another (your rights), and (to) the ties of relationship. Surely Allah is ever a Watcher over you."*

The name and the number of every chapter of the Qur'an is significant. The chapter from which this verse is quoted is titled, *"Al-Nisa –* **THE WOMEN***."* It is the fourth chapter of the Qur'an. The Honorable Elijah Muhammad taught us that the number 4 represents foundation and preparation.

Foundation is defined as (1): The basis or groundwork of anything: the moral foundation of both society and religion. (2): The natural or prepared ground or base on which some structure rests.

Preparation is defined as (1): A proceeding, measure, or provision by which one prepares for something: preparation for a journey. (2): Any proceeding, experience, or the like considered as a mode of preparing for the future.

The people and nations of the world must understand that women are the foundation of civilization, and the preparedness of the woman is the basis from which a good family and a good civilization comes into existence. No female can be prepared to be the foundation of a great society if that female is disallowed the fullness of education, the cultivation of the nature in which she is created, and the cultivation of her God-given gifts and talents.

This verse of the Qur'an opens up by teaching us that our first duty is to our Lord, our Nourisher, and our Sustainer who evolves us from a tiny life germ and makes us attain stage after stage until we reach our eventual perfection.

Duty to Allah (God) is the prerequisite for all other duties. Life without duty to Allah (God) first and foremost is a life that will fail in its duty to self and others. If we cannot be dutiful to Him who created us and gave us a creation out of which we sustain our lives from which we create livelihoods, then, that dereliction of duty to Him will cause us to be derelict in our duty to self, parents, husbands, children and society. So, keeping our duty to Allah (God) is the foremost duty for human life. We are obligated to serve Allah (God). We are obligated to worship Him and to set up no rival or partner with Him. We are obligated to pray to Him and to ask His assistance in all things through patience and prayer.

This verse of the Qur'an under discussion teaches us that Allah (God) created us from a single being and created our mates of the same essence, and from these two He spread many men and women. Then, we are reminded again, *"And keep your duty to Allah, by Whom you demand one of another (your rights), and to the ties of relationship."*

Recognition of Allah (God) as the Supreme, the Sovereign of the universe, is a must because He is the One who created in the male and female our nature. This nature of male and female causes us to demand of each other our rights.

The Most Honorable Elijah Muhammad and The Honorable Minister Louis Farrakhan have been chosen by Allah (God) to lay the foundation for a new world. The foundation for a new world must begin with a new woman. They have been devoted to the elevation of the woman.

We are taught civilization is measured by the woman. If you want to take the world down, the place of attack is the female. If you want to build a world up, you start with the female.

The Honorable Elijah Muhammad said, "Seventy-five percent of His work was with the female." Therefore, He strived mightily to make something of the Black woman. He taught her how to sew and cook, how to rear her children, how to take care of her husband, how to keep a clean home, and in general, He taught her how to act at home and abroad. His desire was to produce a very high level of civilization coming through a reformed female. He took great joy in seeing our women come from a low state or condition constantly improving themselves. He taught them about loud raucous behavior and laughter. He loved to hear the refined speech of the female. He wanted her highly educated, cultivated, and refined. He taught the female how to walk, sit and stand. He showed her, her mother's dressing room that she had not seen in 400 years; meaning He showed her the styles of the righteous women of the East from whom she is a descendant. He loved to see her speaking with firmness to men and never being forward in the presence of men. He hated sisters to speak to men with soft, sultry speech. He taught her, as well as the male, according to the Qur'an, that both should lower their gaze when they are in each other's company. He dressed the female in such a way that men could not know the beauty of her form, but, would only become acquainted with the beauty of their faces and their expressions so the male would not be physically attracted to her alone, but, spiritually attracted to her as well.

The Honorable Minister Louis Farrakhan teaches us that, "the purpose for knowledge is to feed the development of the human being until that human grows into divine and becomes a true manifestation of the characteristics of God." The human being is born with an insatiable desire to learn and this natural desire causes us to embark on the path or journey to seek knowledge.

It is imperative that the female build a proper relationship with Allah (God) first. Our duty is first and foremost to Allah (God) who created us. We are born into the world in debt to the Creator; a debt we can never, ever pay. We must worship Him and Him alone. We must not set up any rival or partner with Him. We must learn to love self, accept self, and know our value and our worth. This is why I have been inspired to compile this book to encourage women and girls to accept our own and be ourselves.

Chapter One

The Woman: God's Second Self

Allah, God the Originator, who created the heavens and the earth, is The Mighty, The Wise, The Best Knower, The Light, The Beneficent and The Merciful.

"He it is Who created the heavens and the earth in six periods, and He is established on the Throne of Power. He knows that which goes down into the earth and that which comes forth out of it, and that which comes down from heaven and that which goes up to it. And He is with you wherever you are. And Allah is Seer of what you do. His is the kingdom of the heavens and the earth; and to Allah are (all) affairs returned." **–Holy Qur'an, Surah 57, verses 4-5**

The Honorable Elijah Muhammad said to us, **"An atom sparkled in the darkness and God began to create Himself out of the material of the darkness."** The Honorable Elijah Muhammad is telling us that matter was there but the matter was doing nothing. It had no form, aim or purpose until an atom sparkled in the darkness.

The Holy Qur'an, in Surah 112, says, *"He neither begets nor is He begotten."* The first God was the Originator of Himself. He was not begotten. The One that comes in the end does not beget. He does not need a son from His loins. He produces a nation from the wisdom of His mouth. He fashioned Himself out of darkness.

The Bible teaches, *"In the beginning..."*—it does not tell you when that beginning was, but it allows you to know there was a beginning—*"In the beginning God created the heavens and the earth. And the earth was without form and void, and darkness was upon the face of the deep."* Darkness preceded light. Now let us take a look into this **"darkness."**

The darkness of the womb is not a shadow; it is real darkness. The Holy Qur'an calls it **"triple darkness."** It is layers of darkness, but, in that darkness is the power to create life. In that darkness there is the germ of light.

The Honorable Elijah Muhammad said the first act of creation after the Self-Creation of God, He studied Himself, knowing it was painful and difficult. He studied Himself and brought from Himself a second self. The female, according to the Bible, is a part of the man. But she is more than a part of man; the woman is the second self of God.

The Honorable Elijah Muhammad told us about a brother who was invited to dinner as his guest and during dinner began asking him about the origin of the woman or the female trying to connect her to the moon's history. The Honorable Elijah Muhammad replied, 'Brother, as far back as the man goes, the woman was there'. Seeking to understand further, the brother repeated the question about the woman's origin, to which the Honorable Elijah Muhammad, gave the same answer. He has furthermore taught us that when God was fashioning Himself out of darkness or the dark womb of space, he proclaimed this production to the second part of Himself as the female aspect of his own creation. She is referred to as co-creator and co-producer in his own self-creation. Thus, she is called the twin of Himself. As he looked at His creation, he honored the entire universe after her.

The Honorable Elijah Muhammad taught us that Master W. Fard Muhammad identified the whole universe figuratively as "she;" honoring the power of the female as co-creator and co-producer and help-meet of God in his own self-creation coming out of the dark womb of space. Our sun is also a star; a star with such magnetic power and attraction that it produced in its sphere nine planets which rotate around her by the law of attraction, electromagnetic energy and the force of gravity that keeps us rotating at the same speed of 1,037 1/3 miles per hour around her solar disk.

The sun symbolizes the procreation, regeneration and birthing process, and in this sense the projected work of the woman or the female in her relationship to God. The 12th Chapter of Revelation describes a woman clothed in the sun and the moon under her feet, and upon her head a crown of 12 stars. And she being with child, cried travailing in birth, and pained to be delivered.

These verses have a special spiritual relationship to the Messenger of God who is also stylized as a woman. This image of the woman in the 12th Chapter of Revelation also symbolizes the solar system the Honorable Elijah Muhammad has taught us represents the Big Ten, the sun and her nine planets.

Herein lies the Secret of God which the Honorable Minister Louis Farrakhan has taught us lies in the woman in her ability to give birth to a child or a god in a nine-month period or cycle of life.

When the female or woman comes to recognize the power she has in the God head to be his help meet, in the creation of the heavens and earth, she will become more spiritually aware and conscious of her great role in the New World Order God is now bringing about in the universal change of worlds.

In the Qur'an, Allah (God) says, *"I created you from a single essence and I created your mate (female) of the same essence and from these two, I have spread many men and women."*

The Black man and woman are created in God's image and after His likeness. We started from a tiny life germ; the one that impregnated the egg you cannot see with the naked eye. That is how infinitesimally small the sperm was. That is how infinitesimally small the egg was, but, that sperm with a little tail and a head had some intelligence in it because it knew where to go and what it wanted to do.

In the dark, that sperm found the egg and the first cell of life began in darkness. But, the cell had a light of itself—electricity inside the cell, a neutron, a proton and an electron. The cell of life was like an atom. The light of itself caused it to start rotating around the light of itself and it began breaking down and building up.

We do not know how long it took for brains to form in the darkness, but, the first thing that forms when a baby is conceived in the womb is not the tail. The first thing that forms is the head. It is the head that calls the arms into existence, the feet into existence, and, the organs into existence.

Before you could think, there was an intelligence working in you that is the Light of Allah (God), the Power of Allah (God). Even before the growth of intelligence in the darkness, we were fashioned out of a tiny life germ—sperm mixed with ovum. We were called into existence by what was in that tiny sperm, the head of it, and, at the end of nine months, we came forth knowing nothing, but, with a capacity to learn everything.

The Bible says, "Love God with all your heart, soul, mind and strength," which does not leave anything for anyone else. Allah (God) wants it all. Then, the Bible says we must love our brother as we love ourselves.

Of all friendships of friends and relations, there is no friendship equal to the Friendship of Allah (God). To have Allah (God) as our Friend, we have a Place of Refuge — we have a shelter from the great stormy tempest of the wicked.

Allah God is The Mighty, The Wise, The Best Knower, The Light, The Beneficent and The Merciful. Since man is what he eats, if you feed from the Revealed Word of God, and live the Word of God, then God lives in you.

Surah 5, verse 116 which speaks of Jesus' response to Allah that *"Thou knowest what is in my mind, and I know not what is in Thy mind."* In reality, the "Mind of God" is the only real mystery and great adventure that exists in life. It is our purpose in life to discover (explore) the infinite frontier that is the Mind of God. If we have the proper attitude, life with all its trials and tribulations, joys and expectations, is a "research expedition into the Mind of God."

The greatest demonstration of Allah's (God's) love is that He would knock on the door of your mind and offer you an invitation to receive Him. His Word is Him. His Word, the Word of the Book, has the power to transform human life. It has the power to give sight to the blind and hearing to the deaf. It has the power to raise people who are mentally dead and give them life.

In the Supreme Wisdom under The Student Enrollment it asks the question.

Who is the Original man?

The Original man is the Asiatic black man; the Maker; the Owner; the Cream of the planet Earth— God of the Universe.

It is man who contains the vital force-energy and power of our universal consciousness made up of the material of God, Himself, and is equated to the very nature in which He, Allah, has created man to reflect His image from darkness into light. We have fallen almost completely from our original orbit from the top of civilization and the cosmic sciences we once knew. But we are gradually coming forth by the will and power of Master Fard Muhammad, the Great Mahdi, who found us in the mud of civilization and is restoring and regenerating us back to full recuperation and health. He has given us, through his children's Apostle and Servant, the Honorable Elijah Muhammad, a full knowledge of God and ourselves by which we are able to relate fully to the rest of the world of humanity as well as to other beings and civilizations yet to be known in our Cosmos.

The greatest of God's gifts is divine guidance that comes from revelation through His prophets, messengers, and scriptures.

I give sincere gratitude to Allah who appeared in the person of Master Fard Muhammad to whom praises are due forever for the Teachings of the Most Honorable Elijah Muhammad and I am thankful for the Most Honorable Elijah Muhammad and the Honorable Minister Louis Farrakhan for their years of dedicated sacrifice, suffering and hard work to raise the Black man and the Black woman mentally, morally and spiritually from the condition that 400 years of slavery, free labor and injustice have put us in.

Chapter Two

A Nation Can Rise No Higher Than Its Woman

The scripture says, *"Train up the child in the way it should go and when it is old, it will not depart from that way."*

The Honorable Minister Louis Farrakhan teaches us in order for the female to produce a great future for us; she must be filled with the desire for knowledge, specifically the knowledge of God and His Word. Any society that deprives the female of the deepest aspect of the study of the Word of God is a society that will not approach the potential of its greatness. For, only when we have a highly spiritual and moral woman, educated, cultivated, cultured and refined, will she be able to bring into existence a civilization bearing these same fine qualities and characteristics.

What is God's view of the female? She is a manifestation of His attribute of mercy to the world. She is undeserved kindness; through her we are extended through the generations. It is only through the woman that we live again, and again, and again. It is only through her that we continue to move toward the true perfection that God desires for His creation. She is the cornerstone of the family and therefore is critical in the whole process of nation and world building.

When a women is innocent, a virgin, and is raised in a wholesome environment, she loves purely. The first love of a girl in a wholesome environment is the male image of her father. She wants to serve and she loves to be hugged by her father because it gives her a sense of safety and security because, by nature, we desire to be made secure.

According to the (Random House Dictionary) virtue is described as "moral excellence, goodness; righteousness. It is conformity of one's life and conduct to moral and ethical principles; uprightness; rectitude."

Virtue is more valuable than increased knowledge at the expense of your chastity because virtue and chastity builds character in a woman. But education alone doesn't necessarily build your character.

You can have a B.S. degree and be a liar, a cheat, and an adulterer so going to school doesn't necessarily build your character.

The hallmark of our educational system should be built on virtue and righteousness along with building the minds of our young people because every time we invest in our youth to build virtue and character along with high degrees of education we are preparing a better future for ourselves than our past.

We have a lot of knowledge but we don't have character and as a result we are an immoral people with a lot of degrees around our neck.

We will lie, cheat and steal with degrees around our neck.

In the book of Romans 12:2 it states *"And be not conformed to this world: but be ye transformed by the renewing of your mind, that ye may prove what [is] that good, and acceptable, and perfect, will of God."*

So if you want a better world then you cannot have a better world until you make a better people, and you cannot make a better people until you make a better woman, and when you make a better woman you have made a better people.

The Most Honorable Elijah Muhammad teaches us that "Civilization is measured by the woman. If you want to take the world down, the place of attack is the female. If you want to build a world up, you start with the female."

How much more sacred is the womb of our mothers and the wombs of our female children and the wombs of the females in our society? How much more protection should be placed on the female? How much more should she and we guard her chastity? How much more should we be taught and encouraged not to violate the sacredness of the channel that leads to the sacred chamber where God Himself works with women to bring about the answers or solutions to all human problems?

The female must never be mistreated, beaten or abused; the female must be treated with the greatest respect and honor believing that she is sacred. The female believing that she is sacred, should never allow herself to be violated, disrespected, and dishonored and must never violate and dishonor herself. If the female will see herself as sacred and, if the males, will see the female as sacred, then, perhaps we can reverse criminal tendencies in our children and bring forth from this sacred chamber called womb, children in the image of God; children made like the Great Prophets, Sages, Kings and Rulers of righteous bearing.

In the book, *"Weapons of Self-Destruction: A Guidebook for Women in the War Against Negative Internal Forces"*, Sister Ava Muhammad states, "The woman (subconscious) is the bridge between man (conscious) and God (Super-conscious). The world is in the deplorable condition it is in today because of man's failure to recognize this fact. He cannot cross the bridge between himself and God because of the absence of the female in the formula. A man cannot get to God except through woman. To find God, we shouldn't always look up high, in the air, because His real Nature is deep, in the water."

In the Bible, God declares, *"Behold I make all things new."* We cannot bring in a new world except we accept a new idea that will give us a new way of thinking and that new way of thinking based on an idea and word directly from the Supreme Being will give us His sight.

Black women must come into the knowledge of God and the knowledge of self and must strive to be themselves, which is a righteous person. God wants to make wise women so they can bring from their womb heaven, for heaven lies at the feet of mother. If women will submit to God and grow in wisdom, they will have wisdom to feed the beautiful minds of their children and the children will grow up like trees of righteousness; the planting of the Lord.

Women must learn how to eat and how to think righteously. Women must learn how to fast so they can discipline their bodies, which will lead to a righteous mind.

Women must keep chaste until God enriches them out of His Grace with a man worthy of them.

This is the value of a righteous woman. She is more precious than silver and fine gold. In fact, there is nothing in the earth more valuable than a virtuous woman. This is the value of obedience or coming to the foot of mother. For, only at the feet of a righteous mother will we learn the heavenly life and bring into existence that which is called The Kingdom of God.

Heaven lies at the feet of mother. "*Holy Mary*" represents a people who are going to be made holy and then produce children that will be gods and rulers fulfilling scripture. The Bible says, "*Ye are all gods, children of the Most High God.*" Heaven lies at the feet of mother—*Holy Mary*, the mother of a nation of gods that will rule the world in peace, righteousness, freedom, justice and equality forever.

Chapter Three

Sista' to Sister...The Value of the Female

Description of the Woman of God

By The Honorable Minister Louis Farrakhan

"And I want to just describe the woman of God for you. See, the woman of God, she doesn't get her blessings necessarily through a man, although that would be nice. But because the world is so messed up, the woman has to find a *direct* relationship with God. Men, if they were naturally in their right order, they would be wonderful spiritual teachers in their home and the woman could look to her husband as a teacher, as a guide. Poor fellow today; poor us. Sisters [are] going to college; brothers in the street. Sister [is] becoming a doctor, a lawyer, an engineer; brother [is] singing songs, brother in prison, brother selling drugs. She has no future. We are destroyed as a people and we need God in our lives.

In conclusion, Hagar was the handmaiden of Sarah in the Bible. You remember? Sarah was old and she couldn't bear children at that time. So Abraham, the Friend of God, went into Hagar and she conceived a child. At some point, Sarah, though old, became pregnant. Now, that's a house where there's drama, *heavy drama.* Evidently, something happened in the house because, see, a woman doesn't like competition. Talk to me, now. I know in that part of the world, polygamy is the way of life, but a woman who consoles a man doesn't want another woman consoling that man.

There's an awful lot of pain in our women because in their life, there's not the kind of man that satisfies the soul. So, our women, in pain, eat and eat and eat and become more and more obese, not because they want to be, but they're hurting and now they don't care. They're not living for themselves; they don't feel that a man is paying attention to them.

Young girls dress in a way to get attention from men, not good attention; but low down attention. But, it's attention. When you have children and start losing your form, and you begin not to care for yourself and no man [is] really paying attention to you, so you feel that, "Well, the heck with it. I'll just eat and keep on eating. So what if I'm fat. So what if I'm out of shape. I ain't trying to attract nobody no way."

"That's the wrong attitude. You should live for God and for yourself. You don't live for a man. You live for God and you live for yourself. And if there's a good man in your life, you can share the good of your life with him. I say this to you, my sisters, because Hagar was put out of Abraham's house. She's running in the wilderness with a baby, and here's a man that's a prophet and a friend of God. He's in the house, food is in the house, but the woman that gave him a child is running in the wilderness with no food, looking to the hills for help. And David the Psalmist says, "I will lift up mine eyes unto the hills..." I think there should be a period there. And then the question is asked, "...*from whence cometh my help. My help cometh from the Lord.*" [Psalms 121:1-2]

So, Hagar had a *direct* connection to God because in that wilderness, He fed her, not Abraham. So, she then could talk to Abraham as a man like, "I know God too. I didn't have to get Him through you. I got Him in the wilderness in my pain and in my hunger and in my hurt; God came to me."

"And every one of you sisters that doesn't have a man but have a connection to God, you've got it ALL if you know what you've got. If you've got a connection to Him Who gave you life then out of His Grace, He will give you a man, but don't look for one! Look for God in your life and the right man will come along, and just ask God to give you the spirit of discernment! I'm ready to go now. I done messed up everybody's life."

"Family, if you look at our women, we are like Hagar, running in the wilderness with our children, looking to the hills for help. And that's why in church, the strongest members are women because they are trying to find that connection to God through Jesus Christ. I was in a beautiful Baptist church in Houston and I was talking about women and I mentioned Mary, the mother of Jesus. And I said to brother, I said, 'You know, brother,' I said, 'would you honor your mother and honor the mother of Jesus if she came in the church? Would you allow her to come up and speak from the rostrum to the people?'"

[He said] "No, she would have to stand down there."

"I said, 'but brother, she gave you your savior. Isn't she worthy to give you a message? She's a holy woman. She was a woman that didn't know sin. You mean she can't talk to a house full of sinners?'"

"We have messed up religion and we have literally dishonored God by dishonoring the female. I appeal to us as men, don't be afraid of an intelligent woman. Be happy that you have an intelligent woman to be your help meet. Not a piece of meat, but a help meet to help you meet the obligation God put on us as men to be cultivators, producers, rulers. A woman by your side when you want to help Christ build the Kingdom, she is your help meet in that noble idea. But if you are not a kingdom builder, if you just want to, you know, feel good without doing good, then I can tell you that you will have lots of trouble in your home because a woman cannot abide a man that is non-productive."

Chapter Four

How to Love You: The God Within

Love. Paul the Apostle glorified love as the most important virtue of all. Describing love in the famous poem in 1 Corinthians he wrote, *"Love is patient, love is kind. It does not envy, it does not boast, it is not proud. It is not rude, it is not self-seeking, it is not easily angered, it keeps no record of wrongs. Love does not delight in evil but rejoices with the truth. It always protects, always trusts, always hopes, and always perseveres."* – 1 Cor. 13:4-7 (NIV)

Every step of your success journey will involve relationships. Whether you are able to develop positive, gratifying, and empowering relationships, to a large extent, determines whether and to what degree you will achieve your goals and realize your vision.

There are four basic relationships:

1. Relationship with God
2. Relationship with self
3. Relationship with others
4. Relationship with things

When the relationships are proper, they are called harmonic relationships. Harmonic relationships are relationships which are positive, encouraging, nurturing, and productive. They result in good health, happiness, love, success, prosperity, and positive desired results. Harmonic relationships are based on truth, knowledge, understanding, faith, courage, self-confidence, and respect.

When relationships are not harmonic, they are based on negative unproductive thoughts, habits, and feelings centered on ignorance, fear, doubt, dishonesty, and indecision.

In the Bible, the New Testament is called the testament of love because Jesus and the apostles talked so much about love.

Your harmonic relationship with God is expressed in Matthew 22:37-38, "Thou shalt love the Lord, thy God, with all thy heart, and with all thy soul, and with all thy mind. This is the first and great commandment".

The harmonic relationship between you and God is one of total affection, attachment, respect, obedience, and feeling on every level of your being—your conscious, subconscious, and super-conscious minds. When this proper balance exists, you are in a harmonic relationship with God.

You demonstrate your harmonic relationship with God by the way you love yourself—by the way you feel about yourself. Love and value must be internalized first, before they can be externalized to another person. We cannot give or share that which we do not first possess ourselves.

Your relationship with yourself is embodied in your self-image—how you feel about yourself. When your self-image is intact, it is based on knowledge, love, courage, respect faith, and confidence. You are then in a harmonic relationship with yourself.

The harmonic relationship between yourself and other people is described in Matthew 22:39. *"And the second commandment is like unto it, Thou shalt love thy neighbor as thyself"*.

To love your neighbor as yourself implies that you must love—have a harmonic relationship with—yourself first, before you can love and have a harmonic relationship with another person. You demonstrate your love of self in the way you love other people.

The harmonic relationship between you and things is set forth in Matthew 6:31-33. *"Therefore, take no thought (do not worry) saying, what shall we eat? Or, what shall we drink? Or, wherewithal shall we be clothed? But seek ye first the kingdom of God, and (its) righteousness; and all these things shall be added unto you."*

When you develop a harmonic relationship with God, and follow the dictates of that relationship, you have a guide for establishing a harmonic relationship with yourself, others and things. Follow that guide and everything you need will come to you. The thoughts, the people, and the material necessities required to achieve your goals and realize your vision and purpose will be yours for the asking.

John wrote, *"Dear friends, let us love one another for love comes from God. Everyone who loves has been born of God and knows God. Whoever does not love does not know God, because God is love."* – 1 John 4:7-8 (NIV)

There is tremendous pleasure in being one with Allah (God). There is tremendous joy in knowing we are pleasing in His sight. Let us strive for the real pleasure of life that comes from duty to Allah (God), duty to ourselves, duty to our mates, duty to our families, and duty to our community.

References from: *The Twelve Universal Laws of Success* by Herbert Harris

Chapter Five

Embracing the New You

"I can sit on top of the world and tell everyone that the most beautiful Nation is in the wilderness of North America. But do not let me catch any sister other than herself in regards to living the Life and weighing properly."
The M.G.T. and G.C.C.
~Supreme Wisdom Lessons

I encourage you to achieve a healthy balance between your mind, body and spirit. "Embracing the new <u>YOU</u>!"
The question we want to ask ourselves is, 'are we eating to live or are we eating to die?'

Knowledge is the principle resource that can help us take better care of our health. Allah (God) the Creator and Sustainer of all life, has given us direction for taking care of our health. However, we live in a society in opposition to the directions from the Giver of Life, and as a result we suffer.

In the book of Hosea in the bible Chapter 4 Verse 6 it says *"My people are destroyed from the lack of knowledge."*

I have defined two words. Food and the purpose of food.

Food- Food is generally defined as material consisting essentially of water, protein, carbohydrate, fat, vitamins, and minerals, used in the body to sustain growth, repair, and vital processes and to furnish energy.

What is the purpose of food? The earth is a living entity, and because all life comes from the earth, life depends upon the earth, in many respects, for support. As living organisms, we are in a constant state of motion. This motion brings about a constant need for restoration, revitalization and replenishing.

We must eat only the best foods that are absolutely correct and good for the body. Eat fresh organic fruits and vegetables; whole wheat bread; and drink whole milk. We must learn to grow our own food and control our food sources. We must find cleaner sources of water.

Most of our sickness can be traced to our rebellion against Divine Law. Food can keep us here and food can take us away. We dig our own graves with our teeth. We eat a lot of pastries and cakes – the kind made with crusts of white flour and sweetened with white sugar; we eat processed macaroni and pastas. These are friends of diabetes.

The leading cause of death for blacks and whites are; heart disease, cancer, hypertension, cerebrovascular disease, accidents, homicide and legal Intervention, pneumonia, and influenza, diabetes, lung disease, AIDS, cirrhosis, liver disease, and suicide.

As you know, our weight is usually taken when we visit the doctor. This is part of a medical pre-assessment routine, regardless of the nature of the visit (health checkup, sickness, etc.).

The weight of an object is defined as the force of gravity on the object and may be calculated as the mass times the acceleration of gravity $w = mg$. Since the mid-1900's obesity has been regarded as the number one health problem in Western countries. In the United States (U.S.), obesity has dramatically risen to epidemic proportions.

Overweight is determined by using the Body Mass Index (BMI) system. BMI is calculated by dividing a person's body weight by the height, squared. Categorically, a person can have a normal or abnormal BMI. An abnormal BMI is classified as underweight, overweight, and obese.

Tom Brody, in the book, Nutritional Biochemistry, presents a solid definition of obesity. He writes:

"Obesity can be defined as a process where fat accumulates over a long period of time due to an increased rate of storage of triglycerides in adipose tissue. A plateau of weight is finally reached where the percentage of body fat is maintained, and where any attempt to lose weight is resisted by a powerful drive to return to the weight plateau.

This definition provides several insights on the duration of obesity. As most people know, this condition does not come about instantaneously. The long duration in the development of obesity points to an abnormal alteration in metabolism. Therefore, some researchers have called obesity a metabolic disorder. This has merit.

Metabolism is the sum total of all the chemical reactions occurring in the body cells. Essentially, this is the breaking down and building up of substances that support the life of the cell, which is the basic physiological unit of life. These reactions transform substances into energy or materials the cells require.

There is more to this, but suffice it to say, this natural and life supporting activity must be sustained, in balance. The body needs what it needs, and having any more or any less than what it needs, potentially, causes the body to malfunction. Imbalance occurs. This condition is either temporary or long-term.

Obesity is a chronic imbalance that gradually registers as life-threatening, as the body takes a new form-deformity. Medical professionals agree there is a genetic predisposition to obesity, as it is with many other diseases. This is not a grand revelation. This is natural to life itself, as we pass our genes to our offspring. Our genetic makeup is contained in the life germ.

At best, this means our immediate offspring may possess the potential to develop the metabolic-related health ailments we have encountered, just as they have the potential to develop the good traits—intelligence, musical or artistic inclination, and so forth that parents have.

Allah (God) came that we may have life and have it more abundantly. So let us practice how to eat to live and follow in the footsteps of Jesus. We have to change our lifestyles; is that right? And according to the American

Heritage dictionary, lifestyle is defined as a way of life that reflects the attitudes and values of a person or group.

According to the Bible, we live in a world called "death." The lifestyles of the people reflect this world of death. This world of death is caused by rebellion against God, who is the source of good and life. In Proverbs it reads, *"There is a way which seemeth right unto a man, but the ends thereof are the ways of death."* (Proverbs 14:12) Most of us believe our lifestyles are correct, and we pride ourselves in the lifestyles we live no matter how degenerate they may be according to the standard raised by Almighty God.

Did you know the simple, cost-you-nothing things like prayer, proper rest, proper diet and fasting can help heal whatever ails you? Proper rest, proper diet and fasting can help the body heal itself of toxins, especially those caused by stress.

How do we get out this cycle of death? First, we must go back to Him who gave us the gift of life and Who is the Best Knower of how to protect, develop and properly care for and nurture the life He has given. That is God, the Creator Himself.

We have to get to the root of the problem. Our stomach is not the boss. The brain is the boss. We have a big problem with obesity in this country. So let us ask the question, why are we eating ourselves to death?

Lack of knowledge; we don't study, and in many cases we are unhappy, unfulfilled, alone, insecure. Because of that we need a security blanket. We live in a hostile environment and we can't solve our social and economic problems. We are not eating because we are hungry, we are not eating because we need the food we are eating because we are insecure. We are in pain and we derive some degree of comfort from the foods we eat. We are not eating to live. We are not eating for health, we are not eating for nutrition. We are eating for emotional comfort and support.

Lifestyle changes, as with any change, cannot occur unless the person has reached a level of dissatisfaction. The degree of dissatisfaction must be intense enough to propel the person to change. Just mild dissatisfaction on a sometimes basis will not do. 100% dissatisfaction brings about a total change. Less than 100% dissatisfaction might bring about moderate change or no change. The latter is what takes place most of the time, because people usually vent dissatisfaction through their mouths, but do nothing to make conditions better.

Change requires effort. It requires concentration. It requires both mental and physical work. No significant changes can take place without discipline. Laziness and mindlessness are incompatible with change. Anything that must be regulated is regulated through discipline. In this context, discipline is restraint against doing something contrary to that which produces the better outcome. Discipline is achieved through knowledge and willpower.

As Almighty God's greatest creation, there is nothing that humans cannot overcome. Obesity is on the rise because many have developed comfort zones. Even so, getting out of this zone follows a similar course. It is done gradually. It is done through a determined and made-up mind to stick to the proper diet for humans. As the saying goes, there is nothing stronger than a made up mind. Too often, we get weak-minded mid-stream and then create false justification to abort the struggle.

One of the benefits of exercise is that we are able to burn off calories. We expend energy during exercise or during higher levels of physical activity which requires us to replenish our bodies by eating food. Exercise could include brisk walking, jogging, weight training, or participating, in recreational sports, such as volleyball, swimming, basketball, etc.

Numerous activities can offer us a way of exercising. Eating properly combined with exercise leads to optimal health.

It is no surprise obesity is on the rise because there is comfort in food. Most of us live under the constant burden of stress. The demand for comfort is extreme, so we become sex addicts, food addicts or drug addicts. Recent studies have confirmed people eat comfort foods to relieve chronic stress, and consequently, get fat.

In some experiments, scientists have matched human behavior with that of rodents. Eating high fat and high sugar foods caused the rats to produce more of a stress hormone releaser in their brains. It is no wonder why fast food chains are everywhere. They serve as instant yet temporary fixes to relieve stress.

Stress-driven eaters tend to eat more sausages, hamburgers, pizza, chocolate and other dense foods than other people do. Also, stress-driven eaters consume more alcohol than other people do.

In an insightful article published in Essence Magazine, overweight Black woman, from a wide cadre of social and professional backgrounds, shared similar themes as the reasons for their excessive weight. Heartache, daily stress, childhood wounds, and job-related burnout were drivers for overeating.

Generally, spirituality denotes a belief in a Being and/or an Existence higher than ourselves, and higher than the temporal plain we encounter day-to-day. In spiritual development, we can obtain the power to transcend the stresses of life, because we are able to think beyond the "seen" and realize we are blessed with this wondrous gift of life. It is through this appreciation we find real comfort.

Appreciation and gratitude are intrinsic to spirituality, and when these attitudes are combined with compassion, we are really in the realm of security and comfort. Compassion gives us a charitable spirit. We will lend a hand, volunteer to help another person, coach and teach children in athletics, music, or counsel the mentally ill. In other words, the apex of spirituality is we are driven by compassion to perform acts of kindness. This supports longevity by removing stress, as there is great consolation in making real changes in the lives of others. Much too often, we are focused on our own problems and pains. In many cases, the answer to solving our own problems rests in helping others. This leads to the final recommendation—change.

Of course, making lifestyle changes require fundamental adjustments in one's current view of life, as well as in one's life activities. We cannot do the same things and expect different outcomes. Therefore, we must arrange a schedule that allows us time to cater to our physical, intellectual and spiritual development. We have to set goals in these areas.

Goal-setting for personal development is often the first casualty in a societal climate dominated by greed. People easily set goals for things that make them more marketable—completing college, taking a course, etc. No doubt, these are important. Meanwhile, moral and spiritual goals are neglected, and these become the very things that derail people from other pursuits.

Money does not bring true satisfaction. Spiritual and moral development does. We have learned the only thing constant is change. Everything changes, including us—at least, physically. We get older and our bodies show it. However, certain mental habits or dispositions become too concrete in our lives. These also need to change. Some need to be thrown out of our minds.

There is no doubt that certain bad, unhealthy or unproductive habits are associated with a climate that breeds obesity and poor health. For example, a sedentary lifestyle is usually associated with eating in the bedroom, on the sofa, or in an extremely relaxing position. Soon after we eat that meal or snack, many of us simply fall to sleep. The consequence is weight gain and lethargy.

Simple adjustments, such as eating at the dinner table, produce radical changes in one's health and weight. Even more, people can determine that they will confine their meals to the dinner table, thus opting not to take the dessert to the bedroom or den, too.

Additionally, many people sit through hours of TV programs without doing any form of exercise when they can easily watch television while exercising. This simple adjustment can produce great benefits. We must discard those habits that impede our lives.

Preventative Care Guidelines

First, you must pray. You must let the Author of all existence into your life.

Second, you must imbue yourself with knowledge. Knowledge is power.

Third, strive to eat to live instead of eating inordinately and improperly in an attempt to deal with stress or to entertain yourself.

Fourth, we must exercise. If you can afford it, get one of the inexpensive memberships in a health club and workout on a regular basis. If you cannot afford a health club membership, then do some form of exercise right in your home.

Fifth, get rid of your addictions. That is drugs, alcohol, smoking and extra-marital sex.

Sixth, get proper rest and relaxation. Allow your body time to recuperate from the emotional stress and physical exertion of the day, and to re-energize itself to meet the challenges of the next day. Relax yourself by breaking your daily routine with some joyful activity that frees your mind of life's stresses and strains.

Seventh, you should spend a little time in the sun and commune with nature.

Eighth and finally, you should make sure you and your families get regular dental and physical checkups.

Let me remind you, the key to solving our problems begins with self-improvement.

Will is the faculty of conscious and especially of deliberate action. The Bible teaches us that the Will of God is the Power behind the Universe; its creation, its maintenance, and its sustenance. Through continued self-examination, self-analysis, and self-correction, according to the standard or criterion given to us by God, we are doing that which the Christians sing of, "Working on the building, laying a new foundation."

The desire to change must come before change can come. Desire must feed the will, and the will of the human being is what empowers us to make the change. God will never change the condition of a people until they change what is in themselves. The burden is not on God to change us. The burden is on us to change when knowledge comes that dictates we must change. We then develop the will to change. There's a saying that nothing is more powerful than a made-up mind. If you are ready to choose health, health can come to you.

Prayer will strengthen the will. Prayer will constantly feed the desire. Desire will feed the will, and once the will is strong enough, you can change.

We need a healthy community to shoulder the responsibility of self-determination. You cannot fight for self-determination when you are at war with your own body and mind. I am urging you to adopt healthy lifestyles, not for vanity's sake, but for the sake of our future, and our grandchildren's future. Without healthy, strong bodies, wise and disciplined minds, we only help the enemy by serving as the instruments of our own extinction.

References from: *A Torchlight for America* by Minister Louis Farrakhan

Chapter Six

Holy Qur'an Maulana Muhammad Ali

The Position of Woman

Spiritually woman raised to the position of man.

This is another subject on which great misunderstanding prevails. The belief that according to the Qur'an, women have no soul is almost general in the West. It probably took hold of the mind of Europe at a time when Europeans had no access to the Qur'an. No other religious book and no other reformer has done one-tenth of what the Holy Qur'an or the Holy Prophet Muhammad has done to raise the position of women. Read the Qur'an and you find good and righteous women being given the same position as good and righteous men. Both sexes are spoken of in the same terms. The highest favor which God has bestowed upon man is the gift of divine revelation, and we find women, to whom divine revelation came, spoken of along with men:

"And we revealed to Moses' mother saying, *Give him suck; then when thou fearest for him, cast him into the river and fear not, nor grieve. Surely we shall bring him back to thee and make him one of the messengers"* (28:7).

"When we revealed to thy mother that which was revealed" (20:38).

"And when the angels said, O Mary, surely Allah has chosen thee and purified thee and chosen thee above the women of the world" (3:42).

Further, where the Holy Qur'an speaks of the great prophets of God, saying, *"And mention Abraham in the Book"* (19; 41), *"And mention Moses in the Book"* (19; 51), and so on, it speaks of a woman in exactly the same terms: *"And mention Mary in the Book"* (19:16). No other religious book has given such a high spiritual position to women.

The Qur'an makes no difference between man and woman in the bestowal of reward for the good he or she does: *"I will not suffer the work of a worker among you be the lost, whether male or female, the one of you being from the other"* (3:195).

"And whoever does good deeds, whether male or female, and he (or she) is a believer—these will enter the Garden, and they will not be dealt with a whit unjustly" (4:124).

"Whoever does good, whether male or female, and is a believer, we shall certainly make him live a good life, and

we shall certainly give them their reward for the best of what they did" (16:97).

"And whoever does good, whether male or female, and he is a believer, these shall enter the Garden, to be given therein substance without measure" (40:40).

33:35 speaks of good women alongside good men, and enumerates every good quality as being possessed by women exactly as it is possessed by men, and ends with the words, "Allah has prepared for them forgiveness and a mighty reward". With God, therefore, according to the Qur'an, there is no difference between men and women, and morally and spiritually they can rise to the same eminence.

Woman is the equal of man in rights of property.

On the material side, we find no difference, except what nature requires for its own ends. A woman can earn, inherit and own property and dispose of it just as a man can, and the Holy Qur'an is explicit on all these points:
"For men is the benefit of what they earn. And for women is the benefit of what they earn" (4:32).

"For men is a share of what the parents and the near relatives leave, and for woman a share of what the parents and the near relatives leave" (4:7).

"But if they (the women) of themselves be pleased to give you a portion thereof, consume it with enjoyment and pleasure" (4:4).

Women in Arabia had no rights of property; nay, she herself was part of the inheritance, and was taken possession of along with other property. She had no right to the property of her deceased husband or father. The Qur'an took her from this low position and raised her to a position of perfect freedom regarding her property rights and her right to inheritance; a position which, among other nations, she has only partly attained and that after centuries of hard struggle.

Polygamy

It is, however, asserted that polygamy and the seclusion of women, as enjoined in the Holy Qur'an, have done more harm to women than the benefit conferred on her by bestowal of property rights. The fact is, a great misunderstanding exists on these two points. Monogamy is the rule in Islam and polygamy is allowed subject to certain conditions. The following two verses are the only authority for the sanction of polygamy. Let us see how far they carry us:

"And if you fear that you cannot do justice to orphans, marry such women as seem good to you, two, or three, or four; but if you fear that you will not do justice, then marry only one or what your right hands possess. This is more proper than you may not do injustice" (4:3).

"And they ask thee a decision about women. Say, Allah makes known to you His decision concerning them; and that which is recited to you in the Book is concerning widowed women, whom you give not what is appointed for them, while you are not inclined to marry them" (4:127).

Now the first of these verses allows polygamy on the expressed condition that "you cannot do justice to orphans". What is meant is made clear by the second verse, which contains a clear reference to the first verse in these words, *"that which is recited to you in the Book is concerning widowed women"*. The Arabs were guilty of a double injustice to widows. They did not give them and their children a share in the inheritance of their husbands, nor were they inclined to marry widows who had children because the responsibility for the maintenance of the children would in the case devolve upon them.

The Qur'an remedied both these evils. It gave a share of inheritance to the widow with a share also for the orphans, and it commended the taking of such widows in marriage, and allowed polygamy expressly for this purpose. It should, therefore, be clearly understood that monogamy is the rule in Islam and polygamy is allowed only as a remedial measure, and that, not for the sake of the man, but for the sake of the widow and her children. This permission was given at a time when the wars, which were forced on the Muslims, decimated the men, so that many widows and orphans were left for whom it was necessary to provide. A provision was made in the form of polygamy so the widow could find a home and protector and the orphans could have paternal care and affection.

Europe today has its problem of the excess of women, and let it consider if it can solve that problem otherwise than by sanctioning a limited polygamy. Perhaps the only other way is prostitution, which prevails widely in all European countries and, where the law of the country does not recognize it, it is recognized in practice. Nature will take its course, and allowing illicit intercourse is the only other alternative to a limited polygamy.

Seclusion

With regard to the seclusion of women, the Qur'an never prohibited women from going out of their houses for their needs. In the time of the Prophet, women went regularly to mosques, and said their prayers along with men, standing in a separate row. They also joined their husbands in the labor of the field. Women even went with the army to the field of battle, and looked after the wounded; removing them from the field, if necessary, and helped fighting-men in many other ways. They could even fight the enemy in an emergency. No occupation was prohibited to them, and they could do any work they chose. The only restrictions on their liberty are contained in the following verses:

"Say to the believing men that they lower their gaze and restrain their sexual passions. That is purer for them. Surely Allah is Aware of what they do. And say to the believing women that they lower their gaze and restrain their sexual passions and do not display their adornment except what appears thereof. And let them wear their head-coverings over their bosoms" (24:30, 31).

Now, the real restriction contained in these verses is that both men and women should, when they meet each other, cast down their looks. But there is an additional restriction in the case of women that they should not display their adornment with the exception of "what appears thereof." The exception has been explained as meaning "what is customary and natural to uncover." That women went to mosques with their faces uncovered is recognized on all hands, and there is also a saying of the Holy prophet that, when a woman reaches the age of puberty, she should cover her body *except the face and the hands.* The majority of the commentators are also of opinion that the exception relates to the face and hands. Hence, while a display of beauty is forbidden, the restriction does not interfere with the necessary activities of women. She can do any work that she likes to earn her livelihood.

The Holy Qur'an says plainly, as already quoted, that women shall have the benefit of *what they earn.* A limited seclusion and a limited polygamy do not, therefore, interfere with the necessary activities of women. They are both meant for her protection and as preventives against loose sexual relations, which ultimately undermine society.

Disclaimer

This is in no way intended to inspire, in any brother or sister, a movement toward polygamous relationships. The Honorable Minister Louis Farrakhan stated, "The Black male must qualify himself spiritually, morally, emotionally and certainly economically, to even approach this subject matter intelligently in terms of its practical reality."

He says, "The Black man's view of the Black woman at this time is so underdeveloped that it must be characterized as filthy. Because of this, the practice of polygamy today would constitute the disrespect of the Black woman through sexual promiscuity in the Name of Allah (God)."

He stated, "The Holy Qur'an teaches that one wife for one husband is better for us, if we but knew. If and when, certain aspects of the Holy Qur'an will be fulfilled by us, we will be guided into this. At this time, however, I warn you: **No one is to enter into this practice, lest we fall victim to the Restrictive Law which is the Reality that Master Fard Muhammad and the Honorable Elijah Muhammad have imposed upon the Believers.**"

Chapter Seven
Prayers to the One True God

"Surely prayer keeps (one) away from indecency and evil: and certainly the remembrance of Allah is the greatest [force] and Allah knows what you do" (Holy Qur'an 29:45).

Our love for Allah (God) is nurtured from repetition of acts of devotion to Him. Each time we pray and draw the incredible feeling of happiness and satisfaction that comes from prayer, our love for Him grows. Each thing we do in His way increases our love. As our love for Him grows, we recognize Him as the True Center of our existence and the Source of balance for our lives. Once we are right with Him, and only when we are right with Him, do we have a hope of right relations with others.

The best way to strive to be upright in a sinful world is to pray continuously to the One True God, whose proper name is Allah, the guidance. As we are generally sinful and easily yield to temptations, it is only fitting to keep up prayer. Listed below are prayers we can say to Almighty (God) Allah.

Chapter 1 Al-Fatihah: The Opening

In the name of Allah, the Beneficent, the Merciful.

Praise be to Allah, the Lord of the worlds,

The Beneficent, the Merciful,

Master of the day of Requital.

Thee do we serve and Thee do we beseech for help.

Guide us on the right path.

The path of those upon whom Thou has bestowed favors,

Not those upon whom wrath is brought down, nor those who go astray.

Holy Qur'an Maulana Muhammad Ali

Chapter Two Verse 286 Al-Baqarah: The Cow

Our Lord, punish us not if we forget or make a mistake. Our Lord, do not lay on us a burden as Thou didst lay on those before us. Our Lord, impose not on us (afflictions) which we have not the strength to bear. And pardon us! And grant us protection! And have mercy on us! Thou art *our Patron, so grant us victory over the disbelieving people.*

Holy Qur'an Maulana Muhammad Ali

Chapter 113 Al-Falaq: The Dawn

In the name of Allah, the Beneficent, the Merciful.

Say: I seek refuge in the Lord of the dawn, From

the evil of that which he has created,

And from the evil of intense darkness, when it comes,

And from the evil of those who cast (evil suggestions) in firm resolutions,

And from the evil of the envier when he envies.

Holy Qur'an Maulana Muhammad Ali

Chapter 114 Al-Nas: The Men

In the name of Allah, the Beneficent, the Merciful,

Say: I seek refuge in the Lord of men, The king of

men,

The God of men,

From the evil of the whisperings of the slinking (devil),

Who whispers into the hearts of men,

From among the Jinn and the men.

The Morning Prayer by The Most Honorable Elijah Muhammad

Surely, I have turned myself to Thee, O Allah, trying to be upright to Him Who originated the heavens and the earth and I am not of the polytheists. Surely my prayer and my sacrifices, my life and my death are all for Allah the Lord of the Worlds. No associate has He, and this am I commanded and I am of those who submit.

O Allah! Thou art the King, there is no God but Thee. Thou art my Lord and I am Thine servant. I have been greatly unjust to myself and I confess my faults, so grant me protection against all my faults, for none grants protection against faults but Thee, and guide me to the best of morals, for none guides to the best of morals but Thee, and turn away from me the evil and indecent morals, for none can turn away from me the evil and indecent morals but Thee.

O Allah, Bless Muhammad and Bless the true followers of Muhammad, as Thou didst Bless Abraham and the true followers of Abraham. Surely Thou art praised and magnified.

O Allah, make Muhammad Successful, and make the true followers of Muhammad Successful, as Thou didst make Abraham and the true followers of Abraham Successful. Surely Thou are praised and magnified.

<u>The Refuge Prayer</u>

"O Allah! I seek Thy refuge from anxiety and grief and I seek Thy refuge from lack of strength and laziness and I seek Thy refuge from cowardice and niggardliness and I seek Thy refuge from being overpowered by debt and the oppression of men. O Allah! Suffice Thou me with what is lawful to keep me away from what is prohibited and with Thy grace make me free of want of what is beside Thee.

<u>"We – the lost founds – should repeat the above prayer seven times a day. For it sums up our greatest hindrance to freedom and self-independence."</u>

<u>The Honorable Elijah Muhammad</u>

<u>Message to the Blackman, pg. 152</u>

Bible

The Lord is my Shepherd Psalms 23

(A Psalm of David.) The LORD is my shepherd; I shall not want.

He maketh me to lie down in green pastures: he leadeth me beside the still waters.

He restoreth my soul: he leadeth me in the paths of righteousness for his name's sake.

Yea, though I walk through the valley of the shadow of death, I will fear no evil: for thou art with me; thy rod and thy staff they comfort me.

Thou repair a table before me in the presence of mine enemies: thou anointest my head with oil; my cup runneth over.

Surely goodness and mercy shall follow me all the days of my life: and I will dwell in the house of the LORD forever.

A Muslim doesn't do anything without God's assistance. This is the path of true greatness. The Honorable Minister Louis Farrakhan states, "Now when one aspires to serve God, The Lord of the worlds, and to serve Him alone, and he states I must add that second part to it. Not serving Him with somebody else, but serving Him alone, associating nothing with Him, understanding that He is singular. He is matchless. He is unique and incomparable and has no associates, has no rivals, or no partners, is above need of His creatures and all creation, is independent of all but upon Whom all are made to depend. When one comes into the knowledge of such Being and commits oneself to worship that Being and that Being alone, that one is on the path of true greatness. That one is on the path of conquering, not some obstacles, but all obstacles that lie in the pathway of man's becoming one with his Creator. So a Muslim, a righteous person, doesn't do anything without God's assistance, praying for His help, seeking His aid."

Chapter Eight

Faith the Grain of a Mustard Seed

The scripture says, *"If you had faith the grain of a mustard seed, you could say to the mountain be removed and it would be so."* [Matthew 17:20]

In the Self Improvement Study Guide The Will of God, The Honorable Minister Louis Farrakhan states, "In the Divine Scheme of things, faith is having confidence or trust in Allah (God). Having faith is having confidence and trust in His Word; knowing that His Word never fails; His plan never fails; His Will never fails. When we put our trust completely in Allah (God) and in His Word, we have the ability to see beyond our knowledge—for what we know is limited."

He says, "Faith can be as big as a mountain. Faith can be as big as the universe itself. Regardless of what you know, you must have a greater faith than your knowledge. For your knowledge is, of a surety, limited, no matter how much you know. But if your faith in Allah (God) is great, your faith in His Word is great, then that faith will lead you to greater and greater knowledge.

Each one of us would want to develop the power of our own being; to use that power to better ourselves, our families, our community, our people, our Nation, the world. We must seek knowledge and we must develop faith. For it is knowledge and faith that buttresses and supports that great Power of Allah (God) in Man.

Faith is the substance of things hoped for, the evidence of things not seen. When we are faced with problems in our lives, it may seem very difficult to solve these problems. It may seem like a mountain in your life but it is not insurmountable. You can conquer anything if you have faith and trust in God.

Without faith you cannot achieve the impossible. With faith there is nothing impossible. When God created this whole universe from nothing, He destroyed the impossible. The Honorable Minister Louis Farrakhan teaches us that when we don't have faith, real faith in God, we don't even attempt things that people say are impossible. But, when you have faith in God, you will try the impossible and find it's quite possible. Therefore, faith in God is key to accomplishing anything in life you desire.

Blessed is the man or woman who finds his or her purpose in life. Nothing that Almighty God created is without aim or purpose.

Article VII. Women's Rights of **the Muhammad Mosque Provisional Constitution** states a woman shall rise as high as her God-given gifts and talents allow her in her own interest and in the interest of her **Nation** within the framework of the **Laws of Islam.**

Chapter Nine

The Soul Yearns to Meet with Its Creator

By The Honorable Minister Louis Farrakhan

The Qur'an opens *"Bismillah ir-Rahman ir-Rahim."* Why seek His Assistance? Because you and I were created in need, and weak! Therefore, when something is created "in need," and "weak," coming into the world knowing nothing and helpless, that individual coming into the world needs assistance. Before you call out for help, help is there!

God gives every new life a "mother" to assist in its development. But woe to the child who doesn't grow up from the "worship of mother." Though when you're a child you worship your mother, which can be accepted from you; it can be tolerated by the God! But when you grow to an age where you understand that your mother is not The Source of whatever she gives, you must, now, escape in worshiping your mother, you are not justified in worshiping your father. You are not justified in worshiping your prophets or your messengers or your kings or your rulers. You are only justified in worshiping Him Who is The Source of your very existence.

You are required by the very nature in which you are created to search for Him. He gives you signs so you won't get lost along the highway of life. Allah creates life, and He makes it filled with vicissitudes and trials and tribulations; this is all a part of the journey that you may search for Him. He is not satisfied to make it easy for you to find Him. He wants you to long for Him. He wants your soul to cry out for Him. And even though mother can satisfy you for a while, mayor and governor and president may satisfy you for a while, prophet and messenger may satisfy you for a while, God doesn't want you stopping on the road for them. All of these are but "signs" on the road to come all the way up to our meeting with Him.

The Soul of the human being yearns to meet with its Creator, of which the essence of the soul has its repository in the Creator. The soul emanated from the Creator, and longs to return to The Creator. Think over these things. God doesn't allow you in life to get "comfortable." He makes it uncomfortable. When you get comfortable, He disturbs your "comfort." When you "think you know," He shakes the foundation of what you think you know, that He may rattle you and shake you so you will keep on the journey to Him. Unfortunately, so many of us that are on a journey stop before we reach the goal.

Climbing a mountain is not easy. Sometimes you have to stop and take a rest but don't stay there. In 1 Kings, Chapter 19, Elijah was up in a mountain, and somebody asked him, "What doeth thou here? You've got work to do!" So many of us long for comfort and when we find a measure of comfort, we want to rest there. But the Soul of man is constantly disturbed. Even though you may be high from heroin, or cocaine or alcohol, even in your high, He disturbs your soul so the reefer can't satisfy; the heroin can't reach it to "comfort" it. Your woman can't reach it; the man you love can't reach it to comfort it, because He doesn't want you to find "total comfort" in man or in a woman. He wants you to find your rest in Him.

When the trials of life disturbs you, when they shake that comfortable position that makes life "easier for you", it's only because God is beckoning you to "come closer".

[The Creator talking]

"Come closer...there is no rest in your companionship with each other because I have made you imperfect, because the very root of the Universe out of which you were made is not perfect; it is groaning as it moves toward perfection. Since you are made imperfect, I can only compensate for

your imperfection by giving you a law that demands your constant attention, your constant obedience.

"I must help you to fall in love with My Law, because My Law", as David says, "Is a lamp unto My Feet. But sometimes I'll allow you to walk in darkness so you can hunger for the light. I will bring The Law to you, my servant' and if you will love The Law, and meditate on The Law night and day.

Understand, I didn't give you Law to burden you, but I gave you Law to compensate for the imperfection of your nature so that you might, through The Law, relate perfectly to me. And through the Law, you might relate perfectly to one another. And in your interpersonal relationships, when you stumble with one another, through The Law, and Repentance and Forgiveness and Mercy, you can find peace with each other."

But your soul cannot find the peace it seeks in your companionship. Your soul yearns for its Creator.

In conclusion, the female must understand the need to establish a direct connection with Allah in order to experience true pleasure in life. She must recognize Him as the sole supplier of all of her needs and the ultimate source of security. Consequently, through keeping her duty to Allah, first and foremost, and establishing a strong connection to Him, she will find the security and peace that is necessary to establish harmonious relationships with others.

As Salaam Alaikum

Atonement

If my people, which are called by my name, shall humble themselves and pray, and seek my face, and turn from their wicked ways; then will I hear from heaven, and will forgive their sin, and will heal their land".—II Chronicles 7:14

Atonement is the seeking of forgiveness and guidance from Almighty God. The process of atonement includes recognizing the wrong, acknowledging the wrong, confessing to it, repenting from it, atoning for it, forgiving, reconciling and perfect union with Almighty God. Please note, however, that the process begins with recognition. Do we recognize the value of human life?

All life is created by God. The human family is blessed by the grace of God to strive for improvement and progress amidst a society and world gone mad with injustice and inequity. Disobedience to the righteous and just will of God has rendered our families vulnerable to exploitation and oppression.

Atonement is the prescription for moral and spiritual renewal. Black, Hispanic, Native, Asian and Pacific

Islander, Arab, and White American families should engage in the eight steps of Atonement.

Eight Steps of Atonement

1. **Someone must point out the wrong**
2. **Acknowledgment of the wrong**
3. **Confess the fault; first to God, then to those offended**
4. **Repentance; a feeling of remorse or contrition or shame for the past conduct which was wrong and sinful.**
5. **Atonement; meaning to make amends and reparations for the wrong.**
6. **Forgiveness by the offended party; to cease to feel offense and resentment against another for the harm done.**
7. **Reconciliation and restoration; meaning to become friendly and peaceful again.**
8. **Perfect union with God.**

Million Family March the National Agenda Public Policy Issues, Analyses, and Programmatic Plan of Action 2000-2008

Made in the USA
Monee, IL
16 March 2022

92730095R10046